MONSOON DIARY

First published in 2018 by
The Dedalus Press
13 Moyclare Road
Baldoyle
Dublin D13 K1C2
Ireland

www.**dedaluspress**.com

Copyright © Joseph Woods, 2018

ISBN 978 1 910251 35 5

All rights reserved.
No part of this publication may be reproduced in any form
or by any means without the prior permission
of the publisher.

The moral right of the author has been asserted.

Dedalus Press titles are represented in the UK by
Inpress Books, www.inpressbooks.co.uk,
and in North America by Syracuse University Press, Inc.,
www.syracuseuniversitypress.syr.edu.

Cover photo: *Chin Tsong Palace, Rangoon*
by Shane Brady

The Dedalus Press receives financial assistance from
The Arts Council / An Chomhairle Ealaíon.

MONSOON DIARY

JOSEPH WOODS

DEDALUS PRESS

ACKNOWLEDGEMENTS

Acknowledgements are due to the editors of the following in which a number of these poems, or versions of them, originally appeared:

Be Untexed; Collecting the water while it rains: fiction poetry & memoir from Myanmar; The Bogman's Cannon; The Clifden Anthology; Cork Literary Review; Cyphers; The Irish Times; Japan Journal of Irish Studies; The Level Crossing; New Hibernia Review; Poetry Ireland Review; Reading the Future: New Writing from Ireland; The Stony Thursday Book and *Windows 20 Year Anthology,*.

Some of these poems were broadcast on 'Sunday Miscellany', RTÉ Radio 1.

'The Wittgenstein Connemara Diet' was translated into Irish and performed in the show titled *Ní Féidir Labhairt ina Thaobh/ Whereof You Cannot Speak:* The Wittgenstein Project, IMRAM Irish Literature Festival 2013.

I'm grateful to have received the support of a Katherine and Patrick Kavanagh Fellowship in 2014 and a Literature Bursary from the Arts Council of Ireland in 2015.

Contents

1

Monsoon Diary / 11
Keeping Time / 13
Icehouses / 14
South Seas / 15
A Week of Sundays / 16
Weekday Stowaway / 18
Greasy Spoon / 19
For the Birds / 21
The Wittgenstein Connemara Diet / 22
Chinese Vespers / 23
Guest in Reverse / 25
Biography / 26
With this Waltz / 28

2

Something New About the Grey Heron / 31
Circuit / 33
Singing Pillars / 34
Entre Nous / 35
Putting Up Christmas Lights / 36
Surveying Someone's Fields from a Borrowed Horse / 38
Taking the Silk / 39
Sounds Familiar / 40
Mirror, Mirror / 42
Driving to Delvin / 43
Suburban Seductions / 51

3

Lives Looking In / 55
Let us fly away to the famed cities of Asia / 56
On Discovering My Deceased Father on Google Street View / 60
Sundays in Rangoon / 62
Caveat Emptor / 64
The Thirty-Seven Nats / 65
Oh the Delta is Dull / 69
A Reliquary for Louis MacNeice / 72
Look at the Lambs! / 74
The Pegu Gentleman's Club, Rangoon / 75
An Ordinary Life / 77

4

Eliza Island / 81
Chemical Brothers / 83
Eternal Rest at Ardcarne Cemetery / 85
Spire or Stupa / 86
Holiday Home / 87
Hill-Station / 88
I Remember a Clear Morning / 89
A Rose from Franschhoek / 90
Like the Rain in Burma / 94

*Dedicated to the memory of my parents,
to my wife Sarah and daughter Eliza*

1

Monsoon Diary

I

Atmosphere in buckets
hot air
supersaturated
with water
will hardly hold.

II

Starts as a gentle applause
on the zinc roof
rising to a fury of white noise.

III

Everything goes silent
the air-con shudders like a fridge
to the power outage
and heat slowly invades
connects you with opressive outside.

IV

Nothing will dry for months now.
In the kitchen all our fans
directed at laundry.

V

A perfume of wet dog will pervade,
not to mention the daytime darkness.

VI

Shoes for which you have no use, grow fur.

VI

Unseen frogs in a constant chorus
grow bullish and bovine
luxurating in their breeding broth.

VII

In every yard and under every tree
hang items of clothing, drying desultorily.

Keeping Time

You sailed off in an unseasonably warm
and brief spring, its loudness extending

to lilies and irises blooming prematurely.
And all about, yellow landscapes of rape

and poisonous laburnum drooping
above dandelions in their thousands,

inexplicable for that time of year.
I resented how the season furiously

presented and longed for your last winter back
and the bitter cold when ice banked

for an eternity and distant fields eluded
and were restive in a Caspar Friedrich finery.

Fog gathered under bare trees
like liquid nitrogen in the Kildare fens.

In Calvary cemetery, Christ, life-sized
his outstretched arms heaped with white,

while a stone's throw away you lay snug
in your cell under a sanctuary lamp

peering out at unattainable whiteness,
attached to an oxygen tank that audibly

compressed like a ball bouncing
in a handball alley of your youth.

Icehouses

It was the summer of icehouses, those discreet
mounds or igloos of unmortared brick
in the planted shade of trees and laurel.
Always near water, preferably a lake
or the less reliable river for the twenty gelid
tons it took to fill one, not to speak of the labour —
burnt hands and cold kidneys the cost of hacking,
drawing and crushing it down so summer lawns
and drawing rooms might resound to its clinking.
Subterranean and always shying away from the sun
two-thirds submerged, a terrestrial iceberg
that might survive its melt for a few years.
Half-filled with earth icehouses revert to their troglodyte
ways, having outlasted the very edifices they once served.

South Seas

Further from home than ever
and drawn to a thin beach
on the far side
of this claustrophobic island

where everyday rains
visit by lunchtime and heat
is a heavy and sodden blanket.
The beach littered with fallen

and decaying coconuts,
colourful crabs disappearing
from sight and scuttling into holes,
making the sand move.

Twilight and the dark
mangrove doesn't invite.
A boat flung in sideways
from the sea with *Cyclone*

emblazoned on its side
and the slight tremble
of closer inspection.
Ominous silence

of the South Pacific,
and yet all day a low subterranean
rumbling as if out there
currents lap against a coral circle,

invisible but hemming us in.
Evenings given over to the flashing
lights of thunderstorms playing
themselves out in silence.

A Week of Sundays

Your hometown, it was agreed,
had been dying of its own accord
long before you took the train

out in '48, and in your last
bedridden winter I sought it out
for what diminished of wild goose ways

to a few hours in the early dark
of a November evening. Searched for one
of your addresses on Fermanagh Street

to be told by the retired butcher –
who almost apologised for having lived
all his life on 'the one same street' –

that there were no house-numbers,
but of course there were, once.
And the brightest things in the street

that evening were the lights
of the pharmacy and the girl behind
the counter in surprise of strangers.

Since you'd left, it was blessings
of the graves that brought us back,
annual penitential pilgrims

and always on a Sunday,
that childishly consigned the town
to perpetual Sundays and concealed

commerce, its sleeping streets
enlivened by the odd car dropping
a gear on the rise to the Diamond.

Or occasionally an exhaust backfiring,
disturbing adults to glance
in the direction of the border

that skirted one side
of the town and atrophied it.
Lunch after decades of the Rosary,

before scattering south since my mother
could never abide the place.
In the northern town of your birth

I tried to place you. Instead
all I kept meeting was myself
in shop windows, stravaging

your streets to the hotel bar
where I was the only customer
and a child at the same counter

did his homework. So little to report,
except for your parents,
the gatekeepers, still high on the hill

in their eternal slumber above the town,
which, we both agreed,
was dying of its own accord.

Weekday Stowaway

Because he was ill I went home mid-week
became a stowaway in the weekday routine
when aged parents hold their own.

Surprised to find him up, reeling open the door,
a few hours on his feet after four days in bed,
his breathing still laboured.

After tea, I washed up to a faint bickering
in the living room, which I now know
as the language of love –

better to be arguing than to be alone,
as the saying goes, a frustration with what's familiar,
a half-century of watching each other in relays

and at an age that surprises those who reach it.
They settle into their scheduled soap
and I draw a cigarette by the open window

in deference to his lungs, and all I hear
is the TV with its volume turned up high.
Our first box, installed the day Kennedy was shot,

was an odd portent if one at all. That news came through
at teatime, and I sometimes think I can recall it,
though it happened three years before my arrival.

Tea is arranged again, for the nine o'clock news.
My mother turns three circles in the search
for a drying cloth, like a sparrow shaking off
a feather; I pluck it for her, from the draining board.

Greasy Spoon

There are times when one can be so infinitely pained on seeing someone all alone in the world.
— Søren Kierkegaard

Not so much
all alone
as someone

eating all alone.
Man in a
Greasy Spoon

where a window
separates,
is always

obscured,
smudged or
relieving itself

of condensation
as he prepares
to eat.

A paper napkin
laid neatly
across

his knees
and the care
he takes

with this repast
and having
brought

nothing
to read,
he stares

at the blackboard
of 'specials'
and back

to the window
that returns
him to himself,

between mouthfuls
his overcoat still on.

For the Birds

Both in your eighties
then and you'd become
his carer, ministering
to his needs in his new
room off the kitchen.

I overhear you
imploring him to eat,
'at least something,'
then assuring him
it doesn't matter.

'He barely eats
and picks at food
like a bird.'
In the yard,
I see her scrapping
his plate into a bowl
for the birds,

a bird herself,
straightening up
her tiny frame
and staring toward
the railway line.

On the flat roof
of the garden shed,
a pair of crows collect
having ousted
the collared doves
she once saw as propitious.

The Wittgenstein Connemara Diet

Now let me be quite clear,
we will not eat roast chicken
or treacle pudding in this impoverished

place, poorer and more primitive
than Poland. No, to coin or mint a phrase,
we shall not take the treacle with us.

We will have a plate of porridge
for breakfast, garden vegetables
for lunch and a boiled egg in the evening.

There will be no variations,
and, as for drink, we will drink
water or coffee. Strong tea disagrees with me

making me shit through
the eye of a needle. As for water
it tastes so much nicer from a silver cup.

Remember when I say ascetic
I don't mean going without food
or drink. All this talk of denial,

I have never denied myself
anything, not even a cup
of coffee if I wanted it.

Chinese Vespers

Late, I answer the phone –
yourself in Shanghai
and you've been at it all night
and returned to your room to empty
the contents of your mini bar
and meanwhile the sun is creeping up
on your side blindingly through blinds
and the chambermaid's knocking
is becoming insistent even from
my side while you're also on the bedside
phone reasoning with room-service
for a reprieve, to put a stop to all
these interruptions, send up a bottle
of gin, Bombay, like a good man
and forty …. Marlboro Lights
and where were we? Heidegger
and of course Rabbie Burns,
and before resuming hostilities
you insist on a toast
and all I can find is a sealed
bottle of Raki put aside like
the bedside book one never
intends reading and nothing
to cut it with, not a mixer
to save my life. I pour close
to the receiver and this pleases
you, it could have been tea
and eventually we drift
on to the same plain
and I recall that morning
over China when I pushed up
the plastic blind to reveal
the beginnings of dawn
and beneath was a range

of black mountains whose
sheer wetness had just caught
the rising sun and refracted it
like one colossal lens.
And now in a mist of one-
second ticks we get to share
that drink across a broad fireside.

Guest in Reverse

You were the guest in reverse,
cluttering up the house
and making your presence
felt long before you arrived,
not to mention the bump.
We took delivery of
your changing table and lost
half of our living room,
capacious enough
to change a baby elephant.
Your clothes, though
new, needed to be washed
in advance. I asked no questions,
and so babygrows fluttered
on the clothesline and were oddly
decorative in their premature
announcements. Socks in rainbow
stripes curled on the radiator.
One morning drinking tea
before work, I took one in my hand
and marvelled at the unimaginably
tiny foot that would come to fill it.
And in the cluttered cubby-hole
I had called my study, the door jammed
on a hastily secreted purchase,
a moulded plastic seat, safe for you
to sit in like a pharaoh being washed
in the great dry dock of the bath.

Biography

To bring you on
we both walked
in Carton demesne,

spotted the first
swallows of the year
and they were early.

Little alien
I'd have sworn
your head turned
taking it all in,

propped up
on the delivery bed
by the midwife.

Ample Tarter,
your narrow eyes
enlivened that dark

and wet morning
outside. Mother
and daughter ensconced,

I descended the
hospital steps
where a two-Zloty coin,

talismanically gleamed
at this big Magpie
and which I've kept for you.

Exceptional day,
the dark veil of which
was lifting

as I took
the train home to sleep,
whitethorn

literally unfolding,
bursting on either side
of the tracks.

With this Waltz

Take this close-mouthed waltz.
  — Federico Garciá Lorca

All belonging to you died in March,
and, bedridden, you shuddered
when you heard the baby's due date,

a shudder of delight but a shudder
all the same. When March came
and went you grew agitated
but balmed it by saying,

when the apple is ripe it will fall.
And so in early April she arrived all safe
and perfect and you let go of the reins,
duty done, a last responsibility seen through.

Laid out in the dining room and suited
for the first time in years, your Caesar
head reclaimed its handsomeness,
and death, as it does, became you.

My mother exclaimed if she could only
take you from your box for one last waltz …
When I got to your dead star, which emitted
only love, I waltzed around its field
my three-day-old daughter.

2

Something New About the Grey Heron

Days after
your arrival home
I strike out
with the red
pram for the first
time you and me,
solo and head
for the canal
on our ownios
of an evening
of the many
long ones to come.

In the direction
of the middle-country,
where your forefathers
were from,
up as far as the lock-
house where the sky
opens, big and western
and the lowering sun
bestows upon us east.

Ahead, the Grey Heron
holds its soft ground
in the rushes,
immobile brazenness,
and I can't help,
on every sighting, uttering
Thomas's 'heron-priested shore',
(you'll grow used to it).

No shore here:
a high seminary wall
flanks the tow-path;
nor lapping, where water
has stilled for centuries.

Up close, the heron
appears as new, its plumage
rinsed through, each feather
enhanced in evening light,
pincer bill primed
and iris of vivid *yellow*
unnoticed till now.

Circuit

The end might well be at a poetry festival
where a combination of performance anxiety,
late nights and swifty snifters could all come
to roost in the chamber of the heart.

Or the liver, long insulted, might shut down
in a single act of its own in the short night
of a ghastly coloured hotel room – worse still,
a B&B with a shared bathroom, and shared with whom?

Was it the overwhelming disappointment
of your last reading, your very last reading,
or a bad choice of poems, or simply just the poems?
The gags between them that fell flat, jokes

that elicited laughter elsewhere but were never
for repeating? Perhaps faint praise
finally tipped the balance, that and total sales
of a single book gleefully reported to you afterwards.

While others read with poise and timing,
like the delivery of a perfect after-dinner speech,
they'll have departed after a robust breakfast
where they'll have dazzled, and be on the road
long before the landlady screams and the doctor arrives.

Singing Pillars

Delicately carved pillars
springing from the same
stone, when tapped with a finger
(but not with stone nor wood)

will emit a simple music
of three or four pitches.
The guidebook stresses
this music is mere accident,

a completely co-incidental
outcome of the crystalline
composition of the stone.

So the music doesn't depend
upon the shape of the pillars,
nor upon the fine and intricate carving,
nor even, upon the *innovative* skill

of the sculptor. The sonority
of these singing stones,
the music of these pillars
is simply a natural property,

a circumstance,
the guidebook tells us,
that the sculptor
was most certainly ignorant of.

Entre Nous

You'd have known of her but most of all her work,
and I never got to tell you how harried she was after
that reading, distracted and flushed, but she kindly
agreed to sign something and crack a characteristically
dry joke in what was a third language for her.

Something of a imbiber about her and vaguely legendary –
– more so in her youth and affirmed later by another
poet in her delegation. A scent of perspiration
ghosted her leaving. She would relinquish
within two years, alone in her subsidised apartment

a consequence of a lifetime of complications,
nursing the bottle and the muse. Acclaim, in the shape
of a sculpted archangel, had already arrived –
presented to her by the Cultural Ministry for her lifetime's
contribution, but it came without, she wistfully remarked,

any monetary contribution. And yet the angel
was granted a place on the mantelpiece. When a trickle
of international invites arrived, she graciously accepted,
and read in rather grand rooms which were mostly empty,
endured the long speeches with good grace and was glad,

however late, to be simply abroad. Then, there was talk
of her most popular poem (a youthful one she privately
disowned) being cast in bronze, until an unseemly dispute
broke out on the radio as to where it should be situated.
In the end her words still wait for the foundry.

Putting Up Christmas Lights

Over the radio
midnight news,
I hear how

a man
has fallen
to his death

putting up
Christmas lights.
Fallen

from the upturned
ship of his home,
fallen

from the firmament
to terra firma.
Man overboard,

a fall
not from grace
but in grace,

as if everything
is in reverse,
as it will be

in the end.
Fallen from
the lofty pursuit

of bringing light
in the long dark
nights to his corner

of rural Roscommon,
an aesthetic ruptured
but not gone

while his half-hung
coloured lights blink
off and on into daylight.

Surveying Someone's Fields from a Borrowed Horse

Arctic in its strokes, the Louth sky that afternoon,
surveying someone's fields from a borrowed horse,
slow, cautious and inexpert. And you, love,
up ahead cantering the lane lightly and in control.

My horse paused to graze and I lit up one of the last
cigarettes of that year while Paddy walked towards me,
bridles in hand, a Giacometti figure throwing shadows
five times his frame, shouting, *You're not in a fucking western, now!*

Taking the Silk

Taste in ties I only now realize
was something we didn't share

as they are spread out before me,
the knots I could never master

except the most basic Four-in-hand
while you would fashion a Windsor

or a half-Windsor to a perfect
bulging isosceles. So symmetrical,

you preserved them for years
by simply loosening and slipping them

over your head. Like little colourful
nooses they enlivened your wardrobe.

You belonged to that last century
generation, more dapper than dandy,

who turned potatoes in the garden
in a pullover with holes

and a tie neatly tucked in.
Now spread out on the bed,

a sea of Gordians and part
of the handiwork that outlasts us.

Sounds Familiar

4 a.m and jolted awake by jet lag
and the leaden moments that follow in a Best Western
in Chicago, it's then I hear it,

low-pitched drone of the long-distance freight-train passing,
like a dull note hummed on a harmonica,
a sound that widens any distance

as I lie listening for more
and already it's gone, its aftermath brings you back
seven months on, and now in November.

Phantom sound, despite a life
on the railway, a noise known to you
through movies.

Our trains rattled differently
or as an American man
once corrected you, 'on the railroad,'

all in the service somehow of movement.
Our house on the hill above the station
and the permanent way

where we were inured
to the sounds of locos sat in sidings
in bumble-bee livery

their engines turned over
every night to the point
we could hardly hear them,

like living in a lock-keeper's
lodge or close to an angry sea.
Startlement then,

came as a curlew
high above our rooftop
in the early hours,

heading either to
or from the estuary –
I could never work out which –

except back then
it was the most plaintive
sound I'd ever heard.

Mirror, Mirror

At twenty months
you stand on my lap
as you peer

into dark Kildare
on the train home;
your reflection caught,

you chuckle at the oddness
of it all in your innocent narcissism.
Same journey two years back

or thereabouts,
I caught my own reflection
and chuckled inwardly

having earlier
seen the scan,
your tiny skull,

and twigged
that the square jaw
had been handed on.

Driving to Delvin

I came to where the road from Laracor leads
  — F.R. Higgins

i.m. R. Dardis Clarke (1939–2013)

Having left Higginsbrook house and earlier
having paid my respects at the poet's grave

at Laracor – how swiftly he followed
his adored Yeats – and recalling

from the family archive and cuttings
the great and good who made it

to his funeral on that January morning
during the Emergency and forever in black

and white, the frost-burnt fields
and empty white road snaking from Dublin.

And now dear Dardis Clarke whose father,
Austin, was one of those assembled that day,

and of course Dardis's odd devotion
to Higgins which took many forms

and included twenty years ago,
his pilgrimage to the grave,

found under a yew tree as he predicted
and the poet prophesied.

And exceptionally for him,
leaving Dublin behind for a day,

always at two with nature
and never learned to drive nor needed to.

Now he's gone too, a genial Karl Marx
always hatted and clad in black,

to become the airborne dust of his beloved city.
I turned onto a road, saw a sign for Athboy

and with a rare half-day to squander
knew I must drive in that direction

if only toward an impulse from childhood.
Cloud maps billowing, streaks of blue,

barely enough for a sailor's trousers,
verges bursting full of hemlock

or devil's bread as we knew it
and the luminous greens and browns

of trees in the midlands at the beginning
of a summer that would break all records,

and one in which I was leaving,
that old restlessness, and again for the East

only this time with family.
Soon, the half-remembered trajectory,

that old route from Drogheda to Greenhall,
darkest Longford and its curious isolation

being in the centre and close
to the mysterious turlough, a vanishing lake

that fills, floods and is drained by the Shannon
and swallowed as a child, my mother's sister,

whom I still think of as a third aunt.
And the third man? My father back then in his Wolseley,

who claimed he could have done the journey
in his sleep, and did once, ending up perched

above a ditch, wheels churning air. Blessedly
on his own, he brushed himself off,

and carried along 'plain sailing'. Fortnightly forays
with never an overnight, except in summer,

a pull towards my mother's midlands sadness
magnet back when grandparents

and even parents were all alive. I'd announce
to them, if I could, that finally at forty-six

I'm driving if not quite legally
and I can almost hear whispers in my ear,

'go and do the test like a good gosson'.
As if qualified to drive you're admitted

to the human race, which is true
for this country. How twisted these roads

still are, which only now explains
that early lifetime of car sickness

and our family method of curing it;
walking ahead of the stopped car

until the motion had worn off
and the head slowly steadied.

You waved back when you were ready,
the car slowly catching up as you faced

into a few more miles of baked leather
upholstery and benign cigarette smoke.

My parents' patience still stays and how
there was never a hurry if you were poorly.

At Athboy, I glimpse McElhinney's
Department Store, another midland

incongruity from childhood, *Why go to Dublin
for a wedding outfit when you can go to Athboy?*

And since no easy parking space, another sign
carries me along, this time for Delvin,

the road dishing out its own reminders.
Only then I recall the crash

leaving Delvin; an L-shaped turn
at the bottom of the hill that almost

took us to oblivion, Tom flitting me
from Mullingar, before Japan

and he soon after for the Middle-East.
A short high-speed slide through rain

and into a wall, the car sizzling like
a big steak flung on a pan and steam rose

as water on coals. Prone, sea-belt lacerated,
I asked him to cast over me,

feeling my insides might be out.
He lowered me onto the wet verge.

Only then, remembered the brown Winchester
in the back seat, swaddled in sweaters.

A bomb of pure alcohol, which I'd brought
from the laboratory, tired of accounting for it

to Customs inspections –
thought I'd wipe the sheet white,

packed it for home as a preservative,
unaware my dissecting days were already over.

It would niggle me for years,
sat in a shed so close to my parents' house,

threatening their peace. Worrying
at a distance and sometimes

dreaming of winter sun igniting it
until I called my father to finish with it.

In Casualty that night, the doctor advised
against air-travel with a depressed lung;

I was gone within the week
and Tom soon afterwards

with a promise he'd see me in Kyoto.
Never to see home again, a brawl in a bar

in Bahrain undid him and sound sleep
from which there would be no awakening.

I searched for something of him
on the internet but found nothing,

a few photos stored and one in the head,
him grinning outside Carberry's pub,

with a sneaky daytime pint,
a half-life stilled in sunshine.

The L-shaped bend has been smoothed out
and my car ambles up the hill

to the main street, the Greyhound Bar & Lounge,
Power's Whiskey on its gable and from where I think

Tom might have phoned from that night.
Once I stood across from that bar, facing down

the hill, hitching home, cross-country,
when a child appeared and, without

as much as a Mexican standoff, cast a stone at me.
I royally cursed the town and crassly invoked,

to myself, its book-burning episode,
a slight never quite shaken off,

and that oddly personified title,
The Valley of the Squinting Windows.

And, strange to recall, its author
was at the funeral at Laracor,

old pals and close. Not so his father,
the local teacher, forced to emigrate

for his son's indiscretion and the catastrophe
of a writer in the family.

Call it one-horse, but this town sits
so vivid from childhood,

and simply passing through –
the Medical Hall with its quartz relief

of a mortar and pestle now sells wedding dresses.
I peer into the interior of a bar,

dressed in Formica, long since closed,
walk the length of the town as if pacing

a long platform where a rattling horsebox
does for a train. Taking in the gaps

between buildings that open to hay sheds
and paddocks, a kind of Wild West façade;

a row of buildings then prairie beyond.
And what has happened here in over twenty years?

Unfair of me to freight its one street
with past collisions, and yet I'm trying to lay

something down, a store to set by,
for the long haul back East.

Start by driving in that direction,
the downward hill, the erased

'Accident Black Spot',
the now straightened bend,

leaving behind a world contained
and lives you hardly knew existed.

Suburban Seductions

But louder sang that ghost, 'What then?'
— W.B. Yeats

Cross-hair of contrails
up there in the blue
out of reach

of the low drone
from the local airfield.
Ecdysis of gutters cracking –

expanding by noon.
Bovine lawnmowers
in relays will conquer all.

In the village, the castle wall
will eventually warm up,
to radiate a surfeit

of warmth that's lost
to the largesse of long evenings.
The ice-cream van

weaving in and out of earshot
has clearly changed its tune.

3

Lives Looking In

'Windermere' etched on a white marble gatepost.
A few relics and leftovers like that. Strolling up the road
of mostly crumbling colonial villas, and what one can glimpse
of their interiors appears hollowed out in black. Rarely lit
they are veiled by dark greenery, brief dusk and disappeared
by relentless power cuts. Rangoon retains some secrets still.
A houseguard's hut, empty, save for a concealed transistor
tinkling what sounds like a Bollywood tune for no one.

He's to be found in the compound staring at the TV
through a window grille, while the family huddle before
a preposterous plasma screen and no doubt the very latest
in Korean melodrama … Thrushcross Grange, wasn't it?
Those two tearaways creeping up to the unshuttered window
of an imagined happy family to find the Linton brats baying,
screaming blue murder, and the dog on the table yelping …

That draughty oversized hunter's lodge you grew up in
east of nowhere, when, with all the men gone to the pub,
you the delicate one settled down with your mother
for a crucial episode of *Dallas*. A bat swooped
in from the scullery and annexed the kitchen
to the opening theme, sending mother and son shrieking,
routed and reduced to looking in from the dark yard
while the bat until closing time lorded over it all.

Let us fly away to the famed cities of Asia

ad claras asiae volemus urbes
   — *Catullus 46*

A mini Manhattan of rusted corrugated roofs.
We settle in to a raw apartment on the sixth floor,
unaware we are the sole occupants
of the building, eerily quiet in the evenings
despite seven days a week of building site
aural accompaniment. Now the din is dying down,
in so far as noise in this neck of the woods
ever dies down; we live with drills and the thuds
of lump-hammers on ceilings, we breakfast
to angle-grinders slicing in the landing
on a Sunday morning while everything
is being built, dismantled and demolished
by hand and carted out in bamboo baskets
on people's heads through corridors of dust.

No one ever complains, it's part of the old city
disappearing and the new one rising, refashioning
in front of our eyes to the ambient and atonal
music of construction. Our kitchen faces west,
and each evening, a clockwork sun slides
with southern hemisphere haste
behind sprouting new high-rises on the horizon,
breaking the sun's fall by seconds.
Home, a citadel of sorts with 180-degree views
of the neighbourhood; high-density living on one side
and, on the other, an auspicious view of the golden
stupa of the Shwedagon, whose bricks were laid

under its thickening skin of gold; one layer by men by day,
and one by celestials at night

Across the narrow canyon, cross-sections of lives –
and were it not for street noise and language
we could almost lean out and converse.
Sometimes, a house phone rings
in the evening, so audible,
it could be in our own apartment.
I see someone move to answer it and later
the unfurling of bedrolls on polished parquet,
which, in this high heat, incenses rooms
with the tang of teak. Our two-year-old daughter
a-bed and under a muslin dome for mosquitoes,
asks that her bedtime story 'has a garden in it'
and later, 'where's home?' as I direct the fan
to her soon sleeping form.

She loves the gecko that moved in ahead of us,
clicking loudly at night like a wren in a hedge
at home, and we are glad of its industry. Evenings
fill with new noises, honking geese in an alleyway
below, kept to keep snakes away. Demonic
crows gathering on the gigantic and shedding cotton
tree at dusk, and then, seasonally, choruses of frogs
grunting then squawking like birds and cicadas
whose shrill rises to our level to the point
you can hardly hear yourself. Nights of wakefulness,
drawn from bed to the drone of a monk reciting sutras
through a Tannoy all night, and peering through the kitchen
window to find another, golden pagoda, many miles
away, ethereally illumined by a roseate half-moon.

Distant pariah dogs howling, gathering into packs
to roam through compliant streets. The night train's
dying concertina note to Mawlamyine or Mandalay,
and times when I've lain awake, waiting
for the affirmation or release of the soft-gong
of our nearest monastery at 4.30 a.m. or the downtown
mosque's muffled call to prayer. Once, drawn to the kitchen
I found the room throbbing with the hum of boat engines
on the Yangon river – a sound that only occasionally
reached us at dawn, having travelled up the empty boulevards,
before the early caterwauls of street sellers
and breakfasts arriving on the backs of bikes,
from boiled pulses to parathas delivered to your door
or sometimes attached to a coloured nylon cord.

Coloured cords that dangle from every balcony,
primed with a crocodile clip on one end
or a basket in which to haul up the matter
of the world; newspapers, mangoes,
laundry and lottery tickets like pinned butterflies
rising while money and letters are lowered down.
And if all else fails, simply step out and clap:
someone will brave the steep stairs and appear
at your door as if by magic. Already, by dawn,
the heat is up (which hardly dropped during the night),
and to leave the air-conditioned citadel is to dip
your toe into the cauldron and chaos.
Heat entraps and, like Shelley's worm,
dissipates, dissuades you from setting out.

All-day scrutiny of the sun, someday we'll exchange
this heat for the cold, wind and rain
our daughter pines for and wish it all back again,
disillusioned, perhaps, by the promise of our own weather.
Right now, a monotony of washed blue skies and water
from the cold tap that can scald by noon.
At street level, a woman walks with a tin basin balanced
on her head, imploring the sky
with her burden of fish tails and chicken feet.
Late afternoon, noise abated, my daughter calls me
to the living room for the faint tinkling of a bell
neither of us can find, too soft for the monastery.
Then overhead, glass lozenges in the garish Chinese chandelier
shake and make music to the latest earth tremor.

On Discovering My Deceased Father on Google Street View

The estate dead
as if some two-minute warning
had been announced

but that's the demeanour
of most of these street scenes;
aftermath of one of those bombs

that preserve property
but erase people or, in this case,
car registrations,

or simply it's a weekday morning
beneath blue-sky definition
and everyone's departed

except for my father,
framed in his darkened porch
under a panama hat on a break

between gardening,
polishing the brasses, or both.
To his left, the garage

has yet to be converted
for his downstairs
phase of living,

and the tall cordyline
waits for the winter
that will scorch it

beyond ever blooming.
But for now, his hat
casts a shade

and it's difficult
to discern whether
he is dozing

or scrutinizing the horses.
Not even the *zoom* function
can clarify that.

Sundays in Rangoon

> *And books give off more nastier dust than any other class of objects invented, and the top of a book is where every bluebottle prefers to die.*
> — George Orwell, 'Bookshop Memories'

for Shane Brady

The crushing sadness of Rangoon on a Sunday afternoon
when the city flags under monsoon and an all-day
darkness and deluge, broken gutters expectorating,

balconies weeping, and walls and gables all mapped in patinas
of black mould where every drain has overflowed to river
the streets and your feet. And it's your nose that brings

you to a bookshop where mildew almost suffocates,
as if every book will soon bind into one lumpen mass,
having absorbed the shelves, sponged up the damp

surrounds and the very air, all bearing witness to nothing
ever lasting here. An hour in, and little of interest;
Successful Poultry Management among the ubiquitous

manuals for the merchant navy, once the only way out
of this country's isolation. No surprises, until *another*
edition of Du Fu, which my elsewhere shelves are full of,

but I'm drawn to the cover of colourful murals
from the Tonhuaung Caves and where the book *Travels
in the Middle Years* falls open, 'the scent of the orchid fades

away … the wicked have not yet been brought to justice',
and *Melancholy in the Autumn Rain*, 'we have not seen
the sun, when will mother earth became dry again.'

Difficult to resist, and made more so because
of the bookmarks: a 1979 ticket to a vanished cinema,
a tiny printed recipe which could pass for a prayer,

two worthless five Kyat notes and a folded page
of yellowed paper with an inked handprint on either side –
one male and the other female? Both hands etched ghostly,

skiagram of their union, and beneath, and written
in Burmese, *5 a.m. Thursday 21st of October in the Burmese
year of 1315*. So sixty years since they separated,

since that morning, perhaps, when one walked out
into the empty streets, each returned to themselves,
the monsoon tailing and, like Du Fu's lone wild goose,
replying to cries that were its own echoes.

Caveat Emptor

Boards curled with *bump to fore edge* of each.
Age-darkened dust jacket, discoloured, slightly soiled
and distinctly grubby. Back strip browned with light
facing to edges of page-block, rubbing along flap folds
and moderate foxing to pastedown and endpapers.

General wear and rubbing to extremities showing
some scuffing to head and heel panel. Edges dulled
and dust-toned, *as with age*. The spine sunned,
slightly worn with creases to lower rear panel.
Worm-holes throughout but otherwise clean

with no tears. Remains particularly well preserved
overall, no internal markings nor owner name.

The Thirty-Seven Nats

Burma is so full of tenanted trees, scared to countless mysteries ...
— Maurice Collis, *The Journey Outward*

for Ko Ko Thett

Thangya-min; armed with a conch in the right hand; the yak-tail whip in the left. Head honcho, Bossman and the only Nat to die naturally.

Mahagiri; son of a blacksmith and known as Mr. Handsome but burnt alive by his brother-in-law, the King, and now left standing on ogres.

Hnamadawgyi; married the King so her brother could be entrapped, ended her life and his, both jumping into the flames together.

Shwe Nabe; met her husband, a dragon, on the way to see Gaudama's footprints, later died of grief at his death.

Taung Ngu Mingaung; suffering from the runs he went to Pang Laung for a cure, but crossing an aromatic field of onions was the last straw and did him in.

Thinban Hla; beautiful in three different ways in a day, adopted by the Rakhine King, died of grief, her right hand forever outstretched.

Mintaya; a King of Ava who, out hunting, came across a Hindu goddess and a frisson ensued; he grew bewildered and subsequently was assassinated.

Thandawgan; died of snakebite while plucking jasmine flowers for the King.

Shwe Nawratha; King's grandson whose servant tried to assassinate the King, accused of collusion and drowned in the Irrawaddy by the King's own hand.

Aungzwamagyi; sent to kill the King for a reward but was himself put to death.

Ngazishin; named for the five white elephants as soon as he was proclaimed King, he soon died of fever and is forever supported by a five-headed elephant.

Taungmagyi; about which there is nothing interesting to say.

Aungbinle Sinbyushin; assassinated while playing with his queen in the rice fields near the eponymous lake.

Maung Min Shin; the son of the oxymoronic popular-tax-collectors; aghast at their popularity, the King forced them to fight each other to the death.

Shin Daw; sent to the monastery for an education and died of snakebite while still a novice.

Nyaung Gyin; an imprisoned Prince who died of leprosy and leans for eternity on his staff, limbs eaten away by disease.

Tabin Shwedi; founder of the Hanthawadi dynasty, his minister persuaded him to move to Sittaung for safety where he had him killed.

Minye Aungdin; addicted to opium and toddy which killed him, he sits on a lotus throne captured on a rare occasion playing the harp.

Shwe Sippin; sent to supress the rebellion, he gambled at cockfighting instead; his father the King buried him to his waist in chicken shit and left him to die.

Medaw Shwesaga; mother of the above, died of grief at her son's end.

Maung Po Tu Nat; the Pinya tea merchant killed by a tiger and condemned to ride one for the afterlife and be the unlikely guardian of traders and their business.

Yun Bayin; a Chiang Mai King, taken prisoner, died of dysentery in Rangoon.

Maung Minbyu; another prince who would die from opium, seen here playing his pipe.

Mandalay Bodaw; a not very good guardian of two brothers who were killed, and he in turn, whilst trying to escape on a marble elephant.

Shwebyin Naungdaw; his brother Shwebyin Nyidaw, his mother an ogress, his father an Indian Muslim; his worshippers won't eat pork.

Mintha Maung Shin; son of an exiled prince, died from a fall from a swing.

Shwebyin Nyidaw; named after impure gold and executed for having failed to provide a brick for the pagoda of the holy-tooth.

Tibyusaung; Lord of the White Umbrella, father of King Anawratha, dethroned by his two stepsons and forced to become a monk.

Tibyusaung Medaw; mother of the King, she died of 'illness'.

Paraeima Shin Min Kaung; stepson of the King and fond of hunting until an accidental arrow …

Min Sithu Nat; smothered with a pillow by King Narathu.

Min Kyawzwa; married the Mt. Popa sheeben owner and spent his sober moments 'in cock-fighting, alcohol, opium and woman'.

Myaukpet Shinma; en route to her parents died in childbirth; the child became King Mingaung.

Anaunk Mibaya; died of shock when she saw her son as a Nat riding a pony towards her.

Shigon; concubine to the King, died a sudden death on return from Aung-pin-le Lake.

Shingwa (Lady Bandy Legs); killed along with her brother by the King for hiding the Shwebyin brothers.

Shin Nemi; died of grief over the loss of her mother.

Oh the Delta is Dull

a whole day's driving
through its pancake
paddy flatness
for the pristine coast,

crossing the Irrawaddy
twice, its broad brown
meander with a white
sandy ridge of beach
down its centre.

Then bridge after bridge
over its many tributaries
and to each its abandoned
sentry boxes and burst
sandbags

and we'll do a whole
day of this again on return.
An expanse of luminous
green, the once great
rice bowl of Asia

and all too occasionally
a row of precipitous
palm trees
breaks
unsuccessfully with monotony.

Small groups in conical hats
crouch in shallow waters
and plant or thin
in the all-day glare.
And those long houses

on stilts, I discover,
are for ducks –
then the intrusion
or overlay of other
landscapes:

Laois, Leitrim
or Hokkaido
competes, exchanging
one flatness
for another.

And with what grace
does it take to live
out here in the hither
and thither bamboo
houses on stilts

that would hardly perch
a large bird without
collapsing,
and to each a bridge
of one bamboo span.

Inside might be pictures
from an eastern Bruegel,
but all I see is *ennui*
and nights of no
electricity;

the romance of the paraffin
lamp quickly fades when all
it gathers are mosquitoes,
moths and silence.

A Reliquary for Louis MacNeice

for Dennis O'Driscoll, 1954–2012

Finally getting your present framed –
it's taken so long though I did make
previous forays, but framers in Dublin
and Maynooth told me it couldn't be done.
Too long and narrow for glazing
at almost five feet by one-and-a-half …
enough glazing perhaps to lid
a medieval saint's sarcophagus.

The framers here are next to the NLD office
and you'd have got a kick out of that –
in the run-up to first free elections –
and the fact that they double as a decent
art gallery, with your love of painting
and your precious lunchtimes paced away in them.

The framer unfurls the giant contact-sheet
of the fifty-five profiles of our beloved
and dapper Louis; a poster promoting
his biography. And the framer asks
if he's a famous writer? 'He is, an Irish one.'
He's only ever heard of Joyce, in Burmese,

which isn't bad, and I point to your Merovingian
script on the poster tube and add,
'He too is famous, the poet who gave me this.'
And it's then I see the couplet,
When I was five the black dreams came;
nothing after was quite the same,

and think of my daughter who's four
and learning to read and write,
so, framing this, even now,
might have to take its turn in the shade.
The framer replaces the poster
in the roll which I tell him is as precious

as its contents, and he writes a date
for collection on a green receipt.
Your unique script, having winged
all this way to a gallery in Rangoon,
waits for collection, your many detonations
of kindnesses still surprising their mark.

Look at the Lambs!

Hoisting our daughter to the top of the wooden fence
we look out over familiar fields and are glad to have made
the great hemispherical distance home for Christmas.
LOOK AT THE LAMBS! I roar menacingly,

but it's only sheep and at two she doesn't quite get Beckett
but will one day. When a fox startles into the field
we're facing, to be pointed to and run the length of a stone
wall in the direction of the lodge, then disappears,

I think of someone dead as I always do on sighting one,
like a visitation from some nocturnal world, and your father,
now four months gone, springs to mind.
But nothing's said as we dwell on the fox's wake.

'Where is he, where's grandpa?' our daughter pipes.

The Pegu Gentleman's Club, Rangoon

> *Nobody but a European could be elected to these clubs. Wealth or attainments or character was irrelevant; only race counted ...*
> — Maurice Collis, *Trials in Burma*

Christ but you'd wonder why it was never torched,
and at the longevity and insect impregnability of teak.

A colonial bulwark or vast houseboat tethered behind
tamarind trees and high fences, you could pass it by,

for it's taken on the weather, been baked
by more than a century of high heat, then drenched

by the rains for interminable months.
Never to experience the cold except perhaps

the pretence cool of an evening breeze
when French windows awn onto verandas

to creak open and closed. Above a cloister,
where a swimming pool once sparkled,

colour unknown but probably blue,
filled in since; bushes and weeds compete,

and a mound of woodchip where rats have burrowed.
Upstairs, to wander through rooms of colossally high

ceilings, stumps of ceiling fans and great Bakelite
switches that must have always been tilted to full.

Porcelain baths, the object of longing for weeks
in the infernal heat, are now half-filled with dust.

A sun-filled, empty lounge where that cocktail
which never travelled, was of necessity invented;

orange curaçao, lime juice, dashes of two kinds of bitters.

An Ordinary Life

Place of purgatory and air-conditioned cold comfort
for that awkwardly timed international flight,

coming in too late or too early. A hotel almost
in the middle of nowhere yet in the shadow

of the new international airport and enslaved by it.
Stays are staggered by hourly pick-ups

and drop-offs. Like a Japanese love hotel,
only this one is for travellers and their short nights.

Rooms never to get quite comfortable in,
ensured by the prophylactic mattress base

and Nazis eternally goose-stepping across
the History Channel; that and the trouser-press

upright in its over-sighted obsolescence.
In the restaurant, the youngster who was part

of the pick-up team has now turned waiter
and possibly cook. I order Pad Thai

and open my book. The desultory few
avoid eye contact, weakened by transit, vulnerable.

'Are you Australian?' someone asks.
I keep my head down, let someone else

take that bullet … 'It's just that I've got all
these Australian dollars I can't change.'

He later shuffles to the door knowingly
as if we were all in cahoots.

He has the air of a lifer while the rest of us
are condemned to be called forth

during the night and flung with luggage
to the four corners of the earth.

But before bed and the truncated night
I take, as habit has it, my bearings,

down a lane of houses
in the great darkness of the city's hinterland.

A no-man's-land, were it not for the great low riders
of the sky coming in. I see them measure up,

lit like UFOs while some hold like immense pterodactyls.
There must be an ordinary life here,

where all the houses are in darkness and everyone is in bed.
Only the house shrines in yards are illuminated

in their own miniature cosmologies. Here is home,
despite the noisy shortcomings and -goings,

and some child asleep is already dreaming
a nostalgia for this neighbourhood.

4

Eliza Island

Atoll of familiarity,
which I'd point out to you

on the map of Myanmar,
in an archipelago of sparkling

dissonance, eight hundred islands
scattering out from Mergui

(itself an island) and across
the Andaman sea.

One of five sister islands;
Jane, Maria, Anne and Charlotte,

oddly inharmonious in a sea
of Burmese nouns,

and in that neck of the woods.
Improbable how the sisters stayed

not least with the regime cartographer.
Real or imagined daughters

of a passing mariner who planned
one day to furl sails and settle.

Later, finding our family holed up
in a hotel and flitting between

continents, you woke in the middle
of the night and fretting asked,

'What will happen to my name in school,
will they leave it or give it away?'

Chemical Brothers

Only last week I heard you had died
in a hospice with no detail to ease its blow.

At 8,000 miles I'd never have made it.
True I hadn't seen you in twenty years

but enquired after you – your brother
at a gathering some years back –

and heard you were still solo, still there.
I held our friendship dear and in suspension,

like the chemical brothers we once were.
After college we interviewed for the same job,

you, the better chemist, got it, which took you off
to the so-called 'sunny south-east', a concept

I never subscribed to and a town
you never liked but never left, until now.

More than half your life lodged there,
something of it must have grown on you.

I searched its name and yours
but nothing came up. A life lived

under the radar, which wasn't like the man
I knew. Unfair of me to intrude now.

Perhaps that's what you wanted –
now there'll never be any catching up,

no making sense of it all or how friends
go their separate ways and time suddenly

shrinks into itself. You were the sharpest
pencil in the case of secondary school.

Lanky, an inordinately thin string of wit
with burning intelligence and hair,

a frightening way with falsetto,
your parodies of Motown pitched so high,

ears might bleed. Magnificent too
in your defiance, taking on dull teachers

and sleeven Christian Brothers
and dismissing them all.

Thus often consigned to corridors to meet
with the Principal and slug it out,

you always won, and in defeat he may have admired you.
Not that you'd have cared.

Your brains pied-pipered a few in your name –
I see you ahead of us all, on infinite

railway tracks of a long summer's evening,
arms flaying, pontificating on evolution,

thermodynamics and girls, and having us all
in stitches with a break for a falsetto dirge

composed on the hoof while you wickedly,
wickedly, wound up the world.

Eternal Rest at Ardcarne Cemetery

> ... *my greatest pleasure was to stop in country cemeteries, to stretch out between two graves, and to smoke for hours on end. I think of those days as the most active period of my life.*
> — Emil Cioran, *The Trouble With Being Born*

The once surrounding wrought-
iron fence has sunk with its slab
into the earth and left two tilting
bedsteads on an acre of alluring
green quilt which has sucked up
to a summer of rain still gathering
below and across the Roscommon
plains like armies hardly distinguished
in shades of black and towering greys.
Underneath, a democracy of dead:
Tommy Maxwell, the MacDermotts,
the King-Harmons and the two
to three interned daily for the first
seven weeks of black forty-seven.

Spire or Stupa

> *What if it should turn out eternity*
> *Was but the steeple on our house of life*
> — Robert Frost, *A Steeple on the House*

Upended steady leg of the great compass,
Ireland's tallest spire.

Back home on holidays and walking
to Maynooth train station with my daughter.

"See that temple over there," she points,
"that was once covered in gold, a long, long time ago."

Holiday Home

The last time my sisters took him
to the holiday home in Leitrim
we had to carry him up and down
the stairs but he was skeletally light.

That Sunday we drove to visit relations,
which we all knew, for him, was the last
time and where an aunt wound up
a reindeer that grotesquely sang

When I'm Sixty-Four. I didn't know
whether to laugh or cry and stepped
outside into the still air and did both.
We drove back the lonely length

of Scarmogue Lough, the pair of us in the back,
an oxygen tank between us as an armrest,
his eyes narrowing on a slope with a ruined cottage
as he wheezed, "someone lived there once".

Hill-Station

To the wooded outskirts we wandered
and in the distance saw the six- or seven-hundred mile
passage of the Himalayas

and its heavenly abodes of snow.
Early December and we'd make our own Christmas that year.
We halted by a kiosk selling everything;

on the counter a ubiquitous STD phone
(I know, and the joke worn thin by then),
and I put a call through. A clear line,

which my mother answered
with absolutely no awe on her end only straight to business.
"He's out of bed and only middling

but he's just put up the Christmas tree
and I'll put him on to ye." His old man's northern-lilt –
so much more pronounced

on the phone than in person – cuts through.
I hear him still, only now he's gently imploring,
Enough, no more of your dead-father poems.

I Remember a Clear Morning

after *The Pillow Book of Sei Shōnagon*

for Richard Halperin

Sei Shōnagon records, despite the bright sun,
dew still dripping from chrysanthemums
in the garden, how, on the tatters
of spider-webs, raindrops hung like pearls.

This morning I heaved the rattan sofa
to the veranda and began some sedentary
birdwatching using the camera lens
for binoculars and matching the digital

images against the more precise drawings
of *Newman's South African Birds*. Without my stirring,
navy, fork-tailed Drongos flitted on the lawn
alongside Sunbird bottle-green flickers

with impossible red disappearing into ornamental
trees. Southern Masked Weavers, meaning
a voltage of yellow with a face washed in black.
A Powder Blue Waxbill washed vigorously

in the birdbath before the outré primaries
of the Purple-crested – and therefore common –
Turaco appeared in flight with its hollow
Ro Ko Ko rising to a strident crescendo.

And, like Sei Shōnagon, I described later
how beautiful it all was, and what was impressive
was they were not at all impressed.

A Rose from Franschhoek

In the Dutch gabled cottage in Franschhoek
which we took for a few days and where
a different rose arrangement was placed
in every room – the most fragrant, a singular red rose
she'd never been able to propagate,
in the window of our bedroom overlooking
a vineyard and part of its frame,
a gable-hugging lemon tree with lemons ready for gin.

Leaving, I placed that rose in the back window
of the car unsure of what I'd do with it,
and after a bear–hug from Alison in her berry field,
a mother's embrace that would later resonate,
we drove down for hours to the coast
through various highland passes which brought to mind
Kerry and the west of Ireland were it not for vineyards.
All three of us hoping we'd see the last
of the Southern Right Whales.

Spring should have been warming the shallows
they were fond of and very soon they'd depart,
but on the pier that afternoon we'd left summer
in the mountains and sky and sea turned ominously dark.
No boats putting out, and yesterday's warmth
gave way to wind, turned Hermanus into any forlorn seaside town,
as we retreated to the shack at the end of the pier,
drank dry white wine and feasted on fish.

Comparing Hermanus to other seaside places,
Clougherhead, Chiloe or Lahinch, that certain abandon
of places in service to the sea –
our guesthouse room faced the sea, recalling

another in Ballybunion, and the mood of both
was of a retirement home. That night a call
came through that you'd suddenly deteriorated,
slipped down a notch from your already low register.

Mother, you didn't know me last summer,
and how could you? Imagine, you now in your room
of the dune-facing, sea-obscuring nursing home,
listing badly, and for how long? Nothing to be done.
Next morning, as we set off again for the pier,
the rose in the car window had turned from red
to black but still carried its heady scent.
In December last year the fortune-teller whose surgery
fringed the Sule Pagoda in Rangoon told me I'd nothing

to worry over for the next two years, but advised,
keep rosewater and roses about me and find time
to spend in a monastery. An hour crossing the bay
and with the mountains falling back, I'm in mind
of the sea journey to Boffin, tracking terns with binoculars,
when a first sighting was called out and a carbuncled back
or head half-reared and then water was blown with impunity,
as we awaited the declarative tail-flip our daughter wished for.

But the underwater shadow we see, I tell her,
is the size of ten elephants and its accompanying shadow
is of a calf. And soon, a second mother and calf are sighted.
Then a fin-flip by way of a wave and we are eventually delivered
back to the seafood shack, exhausted by oxygen.
In the bookshop that afternoon, a for-once cheery owner
notices my accent and mentions how *Ryan's Daughter*
was part-filmed down the coast because of its resemblance to
    Kerry.

I tell him I remember being on the film set,
a village on a hill at dusk long after the crew had gone ...
our first family holiday in '73. I was seven,
and remember catching up with the adults in fear
of being left behind on the slopes of that ghosted place.
Robert Mitchum drinking alone and asking
my now dead neighbour, *Drink with me as no one else will ...
I'm come to Ireland to find myself drinking alone ...*
everyone fearing the pull of his dark star.

Two books 'face out' on the same shelf, and I remark
to the owner on the facial resemblance between Lawrence of
    Arabia
and Ian Smith, mentioning that I live in Zimbabwe.
*That, I have never noticed, but Smith was a gentleman to the last,
and ended his days in a retirement home on the coast here.
Until his dying day, he expected to be called back
to resolve Rhodesia's – sorry, Zimbabwe's – problems.*

At the guesthouse I step out. To its rear a spine of high
Patagonian mountains, around its front the white horses
of the Atlantic; juggling the journey in hand and an immanent
one home, and was I certain I'd said goodbye?
The sun already set, but still gilding a glass-fronted villa;
a painting by an African Hopper, but an African Hopper
might record the visual untidiness of Hermanus,
its townships and sprawl of shanties;
their inhabitants oddly voided from the centre.

At Cape Point, can I be any further away
from your ordeal? A Finistère or *Fin del Mundo*,
and foolish of me to think I'm gathering any of this
for you, or that beauty can quell your faintly
ringing bell down the coast of Africa. Turning here
is to begin getting closer, my own turning towards

lights of old. Your teetotaller life and strong heart
keeping you above water. A missed call close
to Cape Town, and I think the worst,

the family gathered and in vigil, a nurse asks
might anyone be left, *sometimes they can be
holding on for someone?* The phone put
to my mother's unconscious ear, I tell her
gently to let go. Instead of right for Harare,
it's now left for home. You, a walking book of proverbs,
would stop walking that night, and a rose dried to
a bulb of incense, all the way from Franschhoek
to rest by your unassailed ear.

Like the Rain in Burma

The narrow stone pier,
once part of a pleasure
ground, points
like a grey finger
into Lough Boderg
and at its end
I stretch myself out
and lie on the flat
of my back
in an attempt
to soak up any solar
heat where a gunmetal
Leitrim sky converges
with water and only
the faint sounds
of lapping, clucking
gently against stone
to remind us of the
surrounding silence.
Mother and daughter
join me in stretching out
and from up high
we might seem
a family fallen
from the sky and
in that moment
of recovery,
simply breathing,
listening and taking it in,
I ask my daughter
what the sounds are like,
and she replies,
Like the rain in Burma.

Lightning Source UK Ltd.
Milton Keynes UK
UKHW01f0604210518
322897UK00001B/29/P